CLYDEBUILT

A PHOTOGRAPHIC LEGACY

CLYDEBUILT

A PHOTOGRAPHIC LEGACY

DOUGLAS McGOWAN

TEMPUS

This book is dedicated to the patience of my wife Jean and two daughters Lynn and Jan, who have been forced up gangways of various steamers throughout the UK and further, sometimes against their better judgement!

Frontispiece: PS *Jupiter* sweeps into Dunoon in her first year of service, July 1937.

Page 3: The brand new *Eagle III* in her first year, 1910, sailing along the Cowal shore. (Douglas McGowan collection)

First published 2004

Tempus Publishing Limited
The Mill, Brimscombe Port,
Stroud, Gloucestershire, GL5 2QG
www.tempus-publishing.com

British Library Cataloguing in Publication Data.
A catalogue record for this book is available from the British Library.

ISBN 0 7524 3228 1

Typesetting and origination by Tempus Publishing Limited.
Printed in Great Britain by Midway Colour Print, Wiltshire.

Contents

Acknowledgements

Most of the photographs are from my own collection. I am also indebted to the following for the use of their material: Douglas Gray (Alexander Gray Collection), Campbell Kerr Collection, Montague Smith Collection, Duncan McIntyre, Campbell McCutcheon, John Goss, John Anderson, Clyde River Steamer Club, John Innes, Douglas Brown Collection, Richard Orr, G.E. Langmuir Collection, Lawrence Macduff, Leo Vogt Collection, Robert Thompson, James Aikman Smith Collection, A. Fraser, the Ian Shannon Collection and the Iain MacLeod Collection.

My special thanks are due to Iain MacLeod for so readily agreeing to assist with the proof reading of captions and identification of various steamers, piers and dates, ably assisted by Iain Quinn, Robin Boyd, Alistair Deayton and Dr Joe McKendrick; to Eric Schofield, Secretary of the Clyde River Steamer Club for allowing me to reproduce material from the Club archive; and to Campbell McCutcheon of Tempus Publishing for allowing me access to his personal extensive collection and also for his overall assistance, advice and encouragement.

My thanks are also due to those anonymous photographers of yesteryear whose magnificent efforts have survived to embellish this publication. If any copyrights have inadvertently been infringed, there has been no deliberate intent on the part of the author or publisher and for any contribution which has not been duly acknowledged, the fault is entirely my own, as are any factual errors in the captions.

Introduction

The fascinating history of the River Clyde and its colourful steamers has been told many times in the past 100 years through a variety of well researched works by well respected historians.

The pages which follow may perhaps be regarded as a 'photographic adjunct' which will I hope help to illustrate in the reader's mind the colour and excitement of a bygone age.

The photographs are primarily from my own collection but the idea for this book was born of a very fine collection which was given to me in the 1970s. They were taken by the late Alexander Gray of Clarkston, Glasgow and relate mainly to the 1920s/30s period when competition between the various operating companies was rampant and there was still genuine 'colour on the Clyde'. I believe that many of these photographs have not been seen before which I hope will enhance the enjoyment value.

This is certainly not intended to be a comprehensive photographic guide to the Clyde steamers of yesteryear – it is simply excerpts from one man's collection. I have, however, taken the liberty of devoting additional pages to some of my personal favourites. If your own special steamer is not represented, I apologise in advance and I hope you will forgive this personal indulgence! Similarly, my favourite pier on the Clyde, emanating from childhood memories of the 1950s, was Whiting Bay on the beautiful Isle of Arran. Perhaps it was because it was the longest on the Clyde or perhaps it is simply a nostalgic trip down memory lane! Whatever the reason, I have included a number of bygone memories of Whiting Bay pier in the collection.

Although the book focuses on the Clyde passenger steamers, I have also included a few larger vessels built on the Clyde which I hope will also be of interest.

The steamers depicted are in alphabetical order. I hope you enjoy reading the book as much as I have enjoyed putting it together.

Douglas McGowan
Gretton, Gloucestershire
January 2004

Bibliography

Duckworth, C.L.D. and Langmuir, G.E., *Clyde River and Other Steamers* (Brown, Son & Ferguson, 1937)

MacArthur, Iain C., *The Caledonian Steam Packet Company Ltd* (Clyde River Steamer Club, 1971)

Monteith, Joy and McCrorie, Ian, *Clyde Piers – a Pictorial Record* (Inverclyde District Libraries, 1982)

Paterson, Alan J.S., *The Golden Years of the Clyde Steamers* (David and Charles, 1969)

Williamson, James, *Clyde Passenger Steamers from 1812 to 1901* (MacLehose, 1904)

A busy scene at Glasgow's Broomielaw in the late 1890's. (Douglas McGowan collection)

one

The Early Years

A busy scene at Glasgow's Broomielaw *c*.1896. The paddlers *Daniel Adamson* (ex *Shandon*, ex *Chancellor II*), with *Benmore* and *Iona* canting on the river. (Douglas McGowan collection)

Isle of Bute leaving the Broomielaw with a good complement of passengers in around 1895. Originally named *Sheila*, then *Guy Mannering*, she was purchased by Captain Buchanan from the North British Steam Packet Co. and renamed *Isle of Bute* in 1894. She became closely associated with the Glasgow-Rothesay run. *Benmore* and *Eagle III* are also departing downriver. (Douglas McGowan collection)

Another bustling Broomielaw scene with PS *Ivanhoe* in Firth of Clyde Steam Packet Co. livery leaving in around 1911, and PS *Eagle III* to the right of the photograph (Douglas McGowan collection)

The Caledonian Steam Packet Co.'s PS *Duchess of Rothesay* berthed at Craigmore pier en route from Wemyss Bay to Rothesay in about 1922 with PS *Glen Rosa* by-passing the pier on her run from Millport to Rothesay. Craigmore was closed in October 1939. (Douglas McGowan collection)

A pre-1914 shot of Dunoon pier with PS *Kenilworth* alongside and a Caledonian Steam Packet vessel about to depart on the right of the photograph. (Iain MacLeod collection)

Atalanta, built in 1906 by John Brown & Co., Clydebank was the only turbine steamer in the Glasgow & South Western Railway Co. fleet. She was closely associated with the Ardrossan–Arran service for much of her career and acquired a reputation for rolling, even in a slight sea. (Douglas McGowan collection)

In a great cloud of black smoke, *Atalanta* leaves Lamlash pier on the Island of Arran bound for Brodick in the summer of 1923. This pier was closed in 1946 but was briefly reopened again in 1953 due to local pressure, before finally being demolished in 1956. (Douglas McGowan collection)

PS *Brodick Castle*, seen here leaving Brodick in the early 1880s, was built in 1878 by McIntyre's of Paisley. Interestingly, the old double diagonal engines of the *Eagle II* were used in her construction. She was primarily used by the Buchanan fleet on the Ardrossan–Arran route. She had a rather unusual appearance with her two funnels forward of the paddles, deck saloon with alleyways and a poop deck and forecastle but no mast. She was sold for service on the Solent in 1887. (Douglas McGowan collection)

PS *Caledonia* (*I*) of 1889 was the first steamer to be built for the Caledonian Steam Packet Co. Ltd. Constructed by the yard of John Reid & Co. of Port Glasgow, she had yet another claim to fame as she was the first Clyde steamer to be fitted with compound machinery and two navy boilers. She is pictured here arriving at Dunoon in around 1902. (Douglas McGowan collection)

In 1903 *Caledonia* (*I*) was reboilered and the bridge placed forward of the funnel, as seen here, arriving at Dunoon in August 1927. Latterly she became associated with the Holy Loch service. From 1917-1919, she was engaged as a minesweeper on the English Channel. (Montague Smith)

two

Caledonia (II) to Dandie Dinmont I

Built by the world-famous yard of Denny of Dumbarton in 1934, the second *Caledonia* was similar to *Mercury* but with a number of different features. For instance, *Caledonia*'s funnel was larger and elliptical and was placed further aft than her 'sister'. Photographed arriving at Rothesay in 1937. (Alexander Gray collection)

Caledonia berthed at Rothesay in July 1937. She was a sturdy little vessel and was an excellent sea-boat. Initially, she was used by the Caledonian Steam Packet Co. for both ferry work and excursions from Greenock, Gourock, Largs, Wemyss Bay and Rothesay. (Alexander Gray collection)

PS *Caledonia* approaches Largs pier with DEPV *Talisman* having just departed, bound for Millport in May 1959. (Campbell Kerr)

PS *Caledonia* arrives at Tighnabruaich in glorious sunshine in her last few weeks of service, September 1969. (John Goss)

PS *Caledonia* on an afternoon cruise up the Kyles of Bute in August 1969. Following her withdrawal in October of that year, there was an unsuccessful attempt to purchase and operate the steamer by a group of enthusiasts associated with the Paddle Steamer Preservation Society. She was then sold in 1970 to W.H. Arnott Young & Co., to be broken up, but had another late reprieve as she was purchased by Bass Charrington in November 1971, who subsequently used her as a successful floating pub and restaurant on the River Thames in London. Sadly, she was destroyed by fire in 1980 and eventually broken up. (Douglas McGowan)

Built in 1907 for David MacBrayne Ltd, *Chieftain* had a beautiful yacht-like appearance with a clipper bow. She had a triple expansion engine and was used on the Glasgow to Stornoway service. She is photographed here on the River Clyde in around 1910. (Douglas McGowan collection)

PS *Columba*, without doubt one of the finest of all the Clyde steamers, was built in 1878 by J. & G. Thomson of Clydebank for the princely sum of £28,000. She was unique in many ways; the first steamer to be built using steel; the largest steamer on the river and the only one to have a post office and barber's shop on board. (Douglas McGowan collection)

Columba enjoyed an excellent reputation for good catering – just as well, as her passengers tended to be from the 'upper echelons' of society en route to their shooting lodges in Argyllshire and beyond. She is pictured here off Gourock in around 1930. (Douglas McGowan collection)

PS *Columba* arriving at Dunoon on her return journey from the 'Royal Route' to Tarbert and Ardrishaig, *c*.1920. (Douglas McGowan collection)

PS *Dandie Dinmont I* was built in 1866 by A. & J. Inglis Ltd of Pointhouse, Glasgow, for the North British Steam Packet Co. Ltd. Following a brief spell on the Clyde, she was used for service on the Forth and Tay in 1868 and 1869. However, she reappeared on the Clyde later in 1869, mainly on the Dunoon and Holy Loch service. She is seen here at Garelochhead in around 1883. (Douglas McGowan collection)

three

Duchess of Argyll and *Duchess of Fife*

TS *Duchess of Argyll* was built in 1906 by Denny's of Dumbarton for the Caledonian Steam Packet Co. Ltd and was initially used on the Ardrossan–Arran route. She was one of the fastest ever Clyde steamers, achieving 21.6 knots on trials. She is seen here in about 1938. (Douglas McGowan collection)

She had distinguished war service in the English Channel, covering over 71,000 nautical miles. This photograph was taken before the First World War, probably in around 1910, and shows her alongside the pier at Brodick with a number of warships at anchor in the bay. (Douglas McGowan collection).

Arriving at Dunoon, 24 June 1939, returning from a cruise to Inveraray. (Alexander Gray collection)

Duchess of Argyll moving up to her overnight berth at the 'wires' at Gourock in August 1939. In a matter of weeks, Britain was to be at war again and the *Duchess* would be used on the Gourock-Dunoon ferry service and later during the war years as a tender to various troopships at anchor at the 'Tail of the Bank'. (Alexander Gray collection)

With the evening sunshine casting shadows on her sleek hull, the *Duchess* is seen leaving Dunoon in August 1938. She was finally withdrawn and sold to the Admiralty in 1952 for experimental purposes at Portland. (Alexander Gray collection).

One of the most popular of the Clyde steamers, PS *Duchess of Fife* was built in 1903 by the Fairfield Shipbuilding & Engineering Co. of Govan. This spectacular view shows her off Craigmore in 1905. (Douglas McGowan collection)

She was affectionately known as the 'Wee Fife' and served on a variety of routes during her fifty year career. She was normally used for all-year round service and was one of the few Clyde vessels which saw active service in both World Wars as a minesweeper – in the First World War at Grimsby and Dover and in the Second World War in the Firth of Forth. She is pictured here in the summer of 1937. (Alexander Gray collection)

Duchess of Fife arriving at Gourock in 1938 with just a handful of passengers. (Alexander Gray collection)

Berthed up the side of Largs pier in 1948, she now has an enclosed bridge but the canvas dodgers remain, to be replaced with the more substantial wooden ones around 1950. (Douglas McGowan collection)

Another view of *Duchess of Fife* towards the end of her career, *c.*1949. After the First World War, she was employed on the Holy Loch run but latterly was closely associated with the Millport ferry service from Wemyss Bay and Largs. (Alexander Gray collection)

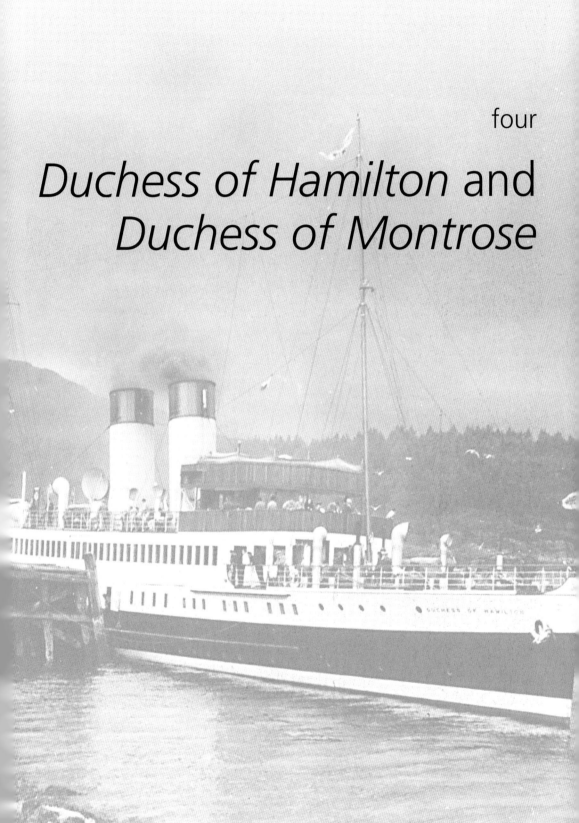

four

Duchess of Hamilton and Duchess of Montrose

A virtual copy of her older sister, *Duchess of Montrose*, the *Duchess of Hamilton* was built in 1932 by Harland & Wolff of Govan and was primarily built to take over from the PS *Juno* as the Ayr excursion steamer. She proved to be very popular throughout her long career. She is seen here in July 1937. (Alexander Gray collection)

Alongside at Tarbert, Loch Fyne, in July 1939, on one of her regular excursions from Ayr and Largs. (Alexander Gray collection)

Duchess of Hamilton did have some notable variations from her sister: for instance, she had a crosstree on her mainmast (added in 1939), a bow rudder and her window arrangement was slightly different on the main deck from the *Montrose*. (Alexander Gray collection)

Sweeping into Tarbert, July 1939. During the Second War, she was used as a troop transport vessel between Stranraer and Larne. Following an extensive refit after the war at D. & W. Henderson of Meadowside, she returned to her familiar haunts and was principally used on the long day excursions from Gourock to Campbeltown and Inveraray as a worthy successor to *Duchess of Argyll*. (Alexander Gray collection)

29

Having given her passengers ample time ashore to explore the delights of the Loch Fyne fishing village, *Duchess of Hamilton* departs from Tarbert for the return trip to Largs and Ayr. July 1938 (Alexander Gray collection)

Manoeuvring off Gourock, June 1955. The flags are up so she is possibly about to pick up a special party. (Campbell Kerr)

Arriving at Lochranza in the late 1960s, on her way back to Gourock from Campbeltown. She is sporting red lions on the funnels and monastral blue hull which was the CSP Company's colour scheme from 1965 until 1969. (Douglas McGowan collection)

In her final two seasons, the *Hamilton* suffered from intermittent mechanical problems and was finally withdrawn in September 1970, much to the disappointment of many enthusiasts. A plan to convert her to a floating restaurant manifested itself with some structural alterations to her promenade deck aft but she was laid up at Greenock's East India Harbour during 1971 without any further activity. Sadly, the plans never materialised and she was subsequently broken up. Photographed approaching Brodick with a charter party, and unusually, about to berth alongside MV *Glen Sannox*, May 1969. (Campbell Kerr)

PS *Duchess of Montrose* was built in 1902 for the Caledonian Steam Packet Co. by John Brown & Co., Clydebank. She was similar to *Duchess of Rothesay* but somewhat smaller. She was originally based at Ayr but later in her career was to be seen on excursions from various railway piers. She was lost during the First World War whilst minesweeping off the Belgian coast in March 1917. (Douglas McGowan collection)

The second steamer to bear the name *Duchess of Montrose* was a turbine steamer. She joined the CSP fleet in 1930 and was very well appointed. She is seen here in 1932. (Alexander Gray collection)

A fine view of a packed *Montrose* arriving at Rothesay for a cruise round Arran in July 1937. She was also used on other long distance cruises such as Ailsa Craig and Stranraer. (Alexander Gray collection)

An impressive bow wave as *Duchess of Montrose* enters Rothesay Bay at full speed, July 1938. (Alexander Gray collection)

Approaching Dunoon in August 1937, returning from one of her long distance excursions. Between 1939 and 1945, she maintained the Wemyss Bay Rothesay service. (Alexander Gray collection)

A well-filled *Montrose* arriving at Rothesay, September 1938. (Alexander Gray collection)

With glistening pristine paintwork at the start of a new season, *Duchess of Montrose* glides gracefully astern up the River Clyde towards her berth at Glasgow's Bridge Wharf. This would not be an easy task, especially in windy conditions: unlike her sister, she did not have a bow rudder and she would have to rely on manoeuvring with the aid of her three propellers. June 1962 (Campbell Kerr)

A few minutes later and now looking upriver, the *Montrose* has almost arrived at Bridge Wharf, probably to collect a charter party, being so early in the season. Radar, the scanner of which can be seen clearly here, was fitted in 1960. (Campbell Kerr)

Arriving at Largs pier, August 1956. This was the year when the *Duchess of Montrose* was converted to burn oil fuel. (Campbell Kerr)

Duchess of Montrose joining her younger sister *Duchess of Hamilton* at the overnight berth at Gourock, August 1958. The *Duchess of Montrose* was withdrawn at the end of the 1964 season and finally left Greenock under tow to be broken up at Ghent in August the following year. (Campbell Kerr)

five

Whiting Bay Pier, Isle of Arran

PS *Jupiter* alongside Whiting Bay pier, *c.*1910. Not a bus or motor vehicle in sight, just lots of horses and carriages to transport passengers to their various hotels and guest houses in the village. Opened in 1899, Whiting Bay pier on the Island of Arran was to be the longest pier on the Clyde. It enabled both the Caley and Sou West companies to provide a much faster service direct to Whiting Bay instead of via Brodick as previously. (Douglas McGowan collection)

TS *Duchess of Argyll* is seen here departing in about 1912 probably on her daily run back to Gourock and Greenock Princes pier. (Douglas McGowan collection)

Occasionally, Whiting Bay pier would play host to two vessels. In about 1913 *Duchess of Argyll* (on the left) is on the Gourock service run and the 1899 *Waverley* is berthed at the southern end of the pier, on a special charter. (Douglas McGowan collection)

An early photograph of the Caledonian's *Duchess of Argyll*, approaching Whiting Bay in the winter of 1908. Not the winter boards in position and her open deck forward. For the 1910 season, it was plated in. (Douglas McGowan collection)

A delightful period piece taken from the jetty *c.*1923. Rowing boats seem to be doing a roaring trade as *Duchess of Argyll* glides into the pier from up-Firth. Compare the beachwear with that of today! (Douglas McGowan collection)

"ATALANTA" ARRIVING AT WHITING BAY.

TS *Atalanta* arriving at Whiting Bay *c.*1930. *Atalanta* was closely associated with the Ardrossan–Arran run until 1936 when she was transferred to the Millport service. (Douglas McGowan collection)

TS *Glen Sannox* has just arrived from Ardrossan in the early 1930s and a fleet of taxis and buses await the large number of passengers surging up the pier to take them to their holiday accommodation. The bus on the left is operated by Gordon Bros of Lamlash, one of the many bus operators on the island up until the late 1960s. (Douglas McGowan collection)

A well-filled TS *Marchioness of Graham* arriving on a summer Saturday in 1937. (Alexander Gray collection)

TS *Glen Sannox* alongside Whiting Bay pier on 5 September 1952, awaiting her next turn of duty back to Ardrossan. The introduction of the new car ferry *Glen Sannox* in 1957, concentrated traffic on Brodick and probably sounded the death knell for Whiting Bay. (Douglas McGowan collection)

Another view of *Glen Sannox* alongside the pier taken a year later (11 September 1953). In the final years, Whiting Bay had only twice-weekly calls from the Arran via the Kyles steamer and relief sailings by *Caledonia* from Ardrossan on busy Saturdays during the peak summer season. The pier was finally closed at the end of the 1962 season and was demolished two years later. There is no physical evidence of its existence today. (Douglas McGowan collection)

six

Duchess of Rothesay
to *Ivanoe*

PS *Duchess of Fife* was the first paddler to be built by J. & G. Thomson of Clydebank. She entered service in 1895 for the Caledonian Steam Packet Co. firstly on the Ardrossan-Arran route and later she was transferred to the Gourock-Wemyss Bay-Rothesay service. Thereafter, she was to be regularly seen on the Gourock-Arran via the Kyles run whilst assisting as required on the Wemyss Bay-Rothesay commuter traffic. She was known as the 'cock of the walk' as she was the fasteste paddler on the commuter runs and she carried a small weathercock at her masthead to prove it! During the First World War, she was engaged as a minesweeper and had distinguished service, assisting in the rescue of fifteen ships and sweeping more than 500 mines. (Douglas McGowan collection)

Duchess of Rothesay sailing along the Cowal shore, July 1938. (Alexander Gray collection)

In Rothesay Bay in the late 1920s. *Duchess of Rothesay* was the victim of apparent carelessness prior to being reconditioned in 1919 at the end of the war. She sank at her berth at Merklands Wharf, Glasgow, as the result of a sea-cock being left open. Despite serious water damage, she was successfully raised some weeks later and rejoined the fleet in 1920. (Douglas McGowan collection)

Leaving Rothesay, May 1937. The flags may be to celebrate the Coronation of King George VI. (Douglas McGowan collection)

Another summer 1937 view of the *Rothesay* as she cruises along the Argyllshire shore. (Alexander Gray collection)

Not a passenger in sight as *Duchess of Rothesay* awaits her next turn of duty alongside a cobbled Gourock pier in August 1938. (Alexander Gray collection)

Her second period of war service came in October 1939 when she was used by the Admiralty for minesweeping duties on the Clyde and in Dover. At the end of the war, she was sold to Holland for scrapping. Thus ended a long (fifty-one years) and distinguished career of a very fine steamer. (Alexander Gray collection)

Eagle II of 1864 was built by Charles Connell & Co. for Captain Buchanan principally for the Glasgow-Rothesay service. Seen here at the old Gourock Quay in 1871. (Douglas McGowan collection)

Eagle III arrives at Dunoon, July 1937. Built by Napier & Miller in 1910 for Buchanan Steamers, she was initially somewhat unstable but this was corrected and she soon established herself as a very successful member of the fleet. (Alexander Gray collection)

On return to the Clyde in 1920, *Eagle III*'s bridge was moved forward and she was extensively reconditioned. She was a regular sight on the 11 a.m. service from the Broomielaw to Rothesay. In 1936, she regularly sailed to Lochgoilhead from Glasgow. She is photographed here on a busy day in 1936 at the Broomielaw when both she and one of the *Duchesses*, berthed astern, were on charter to special parties. (Campbell McCutcheon collection)

Eagle III leaving Glasgow with a good complement of passengers in the early 1930s. After assisting in the Dunkirk evacuation of the First World War, she was broken up at Smith & Houston, Port Glasgow, in 1946. (Alexander Gray collection)

PS *Fusilier* was built in 1888 for David MacBrayne Ltd for excursion services from Oban. Driven by a single cylinder and crank with a haystack boiler, she was not unattractive with her distinctive clipper bow. She was sold for further service on the Firth of Forth in 1934. (Douglas McGowan collection)

A busy scene at Greenock's East India Harbour in the 1920s. *Fusilier* is nearest the camera and a number of men can be seen working aboard, including a painter putting the finishing touches to the white line on her starboard bow. TS *Atalanta* is berthed behind her while TS *Duchess of Argyll* is having her annual overhaul in James Lamont & Co.'s dry dock, in preparation for the start of yet another season. (Campbell McCutcheon collection)

PS *Galatea* (1889) was built for the Caledonian Steam Packet Co. and, with her beautiful lines, proved to be popular. She had a very short Clyde career, however, being sold to Italian owners in 1906. It appears that her engine was simply too powerful for the hull and her speed was adversely affected. (Douglas McGowan collection)

Conversely, PS *Glencoe*, built in 1846, had an amazingly long career of eighty-five years. She entered service on the Glasgow-Stornoway service as the *Mary Jane* and was sold to Hutcheson's in 1857 for the Glasgow-Inveraray run. She was renamed *Glencoe* in 1875 and this robust little paddler was used on a variety of West Highland and Clyde routes. (Douglas McGowan collection)

PS *Glenmore* (1895) was the first steamer built specifically for Captain John Williamson's Rothesay and Kyles traffic. She was certainly not known for her speed and was sold for service in Siberia after only one season. (Douglas McGowan collection)

PS *Glenmore* at Campbeltown, 1895. (Douglas McGowan collection)

Added to the Glasgow & South Western Railway Co. fleet in 1893, PS *Glen Rosa* was a useful little vessel, built with slightly greater draught than others of her size. Following war service, she was transferred to the Caledonian Steam Packet Co. in 1938 and broken up in the following year. She is photographed here in Rothesay Bay, 1938. (Alexander Gray collection)

PS *Glen Sannox* leaving Ardrossan in 1924. The *Sannox* was really the G&SWR's answer to the Caley's flier *Duchess of Hamilton* and like the *Hamilton*, she was a very distinctive and elegant steamer with her tall red and black funnels. She had been transferred to the LMS Railway Co. the previous year but did not survive much longer and was broken up at Port Glasgow in 1925. Although fast (19.2 knots), she had proved very expensive to run and this factor probably contributed to her comparatively early demise. Douglas McGowan collection)

TS *Glen Sannox* (1925) was built by Denny of Dumbarton to take over from her illustrious predecessor of the same name and she too was to spend much of her career on the Ardrossan–Arran service. Originally owned by the LMS Railway Co., she was transferred in 1936 to the CSP Co. to enable her to call at Campbeltown. This view was taken in Brodick Bay on 13 September 1947. (Douglas McGowan collection)

Glen Sannox was primarily used from 1936 on the summer-only Whiting Bay and Campbeltown service. In her final years, her aft promenade deck was strengthened to enable her to carry cars to the island. Towards the end of her career, the *Sannox* is seen here gathering speed as she leaves Ardrossan for Whiting Bay, August 1950. (Campbell Kerr)

TS *Glen Sannox* casting off from Dunoon in 1949. She now has an enclosed wheelhouse but the old canvas dodgers remain. (Clyde River Steamer Club)

The *Sannox* gets up a full head of steam as she goes astern out of Ardrossan Harbour, August 1950. Three years later, she was laid up and sold for scrap the following year. (Campbell Kerr)

PS *Iona* (1864) was a very popular MacBrayne steamer of her time, known and admired wherever she sailed. She was a handsome vessel, with her curved slanting bow and alleyways extending continuously around her deck saloons. When built, she was placed on the Ardrishaig run, then she was transferred to Oban operating from Corpach to Crinan and returning to the Clyde in 1885. She is seen here arriving at Rothesay in 1935. (Alexander Gray collection)

PS *Iona* at Lochgoilhead in the early 1930s. She was broken up by W.H. Arnott Young & Co. at Dalmuir in 1936. (Douglas McGowan collection)

Built by T.B. Seath & Co. of Rutherglen, Glasgow in 1892 for Williamson-Buchanan Steamers, PS *Isle of Arran* was at first placed on the Arran route then transferred to the Broomielaw–Rothesay station. She was broken up in 1936. (Douglas McGowan collection)

PS *Isle of Bute* on the River Clyde in the early 1900s. Captain Buchanan purchased the North British Railway Co. steamer *Guy Mannering* (formerly *Sheila*) and renamed her *Isle of Bute*. She was used for the Rothesay service until sold to a Morecambe operator in 1912. (Campbell McCutcheon collection)

PS *Ivanhoe* was built in 1880 for the Frith of Clyde Steam Packet Co. and was unique in that she was operated as a strict teetotal vessel, no alcoholic beverages being sold on board. (Douglas McGowan collection)

In her early years, she was to be seen mainly on the Arran via Kyles run. An attractive steamer, she was acquired by the Caledonian Steam Packet Co. in 1897. In 1911, she was sold again to a private company with a name very similar to that of her first owners, the First of Clyde Steam Packet Co. Ltd. Latterly, she passed into the ownership of Turbine Steamers Ltd in 1914. She is seen here of Craigmore in 1902. (Campbell McCutcheon collection)

An early view of *Ivanhoe*, in the 1880s, anchored off the village of Corrie on the Isle of Arran. Passengers are being ferried ashore in small boats. She was disposed of in 1920. (Douglas McGowan collection)

seven

Jeanie Deans and *Juno*

The second *Jeanie Deans* was built by Fairfield Shipbuilding & Engineering Co. of Govan in 1931 for the London & North Eastern Railway Co. and was significantly larger than previous steamers based at Craigendoran. She soon became a favourite with the travelling public and acquired a reputation for speed, having achieved over 18 knots on trials. This view shows her arriving at Rothesay in the early 1930s. (Clyde River Steamer Club)

Some years later and on this occasion, the *Jeanie* is arriving at Rothesay in August 1937. Her triple expansion engines had not been seen before on a Clyde steamer. In 1939, she was 'called up' by the Admiralty, being used mainly for minesweeping duties at Milford Haven. Although she suffered from shrapnel damage on the Thames in 1941, she survived the experience and eventually returned to the Clyde in 1945. (Alexander Gray collection)

Following an extensive refit in 1945 by A. & J. Inglis Ltd when she was fitted with new, larger elliptical funnels, deck shelters, boat decks and a mainmast (as seen here in 1946), she was placed on excursions from Craigendoran to Arrochar, Round Bute, Kyles of Bute and Round the Lochs. (Alexander Gray collection)

PS *Jeanie Deans* leaving Dunoon with a good complement of passengers on a Round Bute cruise in August 1953. (Campbell Kerr collection)

PS *Jeanie Deans* leaving Gourock for an afternoon cruise to the Kyles of Bute in July 1958. (John Innes)

At the end of a long day in June 1962, the *Jeanie* basks in the evening sunlight at Craigendoran. (Campbell Kerr)

Jeanie Deans was withdrawn at the end of the 1964 season (along with *Duchess of Montrose*) and laid up in the Albert Harbour, Greenock where she lay until November 1965. Seen here leaving Gourock, July 1962. (Campbell Kerr)

Left: Jeanie Deans was purchased and sold to a group of London enthusiasts who set up the Coastal Steam Packet Co. Ltd. She is photographed here, windows boarded up, arriving at Stranraer for water and bunkers in November, 1965. Her name was changed to *Queen of the South* and she entered service on a variety of excursions from Tower Pier London to Southend, Clacton and Whitstable in May 1966. Sadly, despite a further attempt in 1967, the brave venture was unsuccessful and the steamer sailed only on a few occasions, a victim of mechanical problems and inexperience. (Douglas McGowan collection)

Below: PS *Juno* alongside Rothesay pier in 1923. She was a very sturdy paddler, built for service in the sometimes exposed conditions of the lower Firth, such as cruising from Ayr Harbour. Apart from *Glen Sannox*, *Juno* was significantly larger than any other vessel in the Glasgow and South Western fleet. (Douglas McGowan collection)

PS *Juno* (1937), the second paddle steamer to bear that name, was a sister-ship to *Jupiter*, launched in the same year. They were similar in appearance, the only difference being in the internal furnishings. This view shows her arriving at Rothesay in June 1938. (Alexander Gray collection)

PS *Juno* off Hunter's Quay on 3 September 1938. (Alexander Gray collection)

PS *Juno* berthed alongside Rothesay pier in the 1930s. Sadly, *Juno*'s career was very short-lived. Later as HMS *Helvellyn*, she served as a minesweeper but was sunk during the London blitz of March 1941. (Campbell McCutcheon collection)

1 PS *Marmion* leaving Dunoon pier in the late 1930s in the striking colours of the LNER. (Douglas McGowan collection)

2 The Caledonian Steam Packet Company's TS *Duchess of Montrose* arriving at Dunoon, *c.*1935. (Douglas McGowan collection)

3 MacBrayne's magnificent TS *Saint Columba* at Dunoon in August 1937. (Douglas McGowan collection)

4 Some twenty years later and another striking view of *Saint Columba* returning to Gourock in her final season, 1958. (Douglas McGowan collection)

5 Glasgow's Broomielaw in 1949. TS *King Edward* sets off down the river on her regular 11 a.m. daily excursion to Rothesay and the Kyles. Only three years later, she was to be sold and broken up at Troon. (Robert Thompson)

6 TS *Duchess of Argyll* leaving Rothesay in 1950. (Clyde River Steamer Club)

7 A busy TS *Marchioness Of Graham* arriving at Brodick from Ardrossan, *c*.1954. (Douglas McGowan collection)

8 It's Spring 1953 at Balloch, Loch Lomond and PS *Prince Edward* (built by A & J Inglis in 1911) is being prepared for her penultimate season. She is raising steam, a ladder is placed against her funnel and a small boat is moored aft of her port sponson as painting is completed. The brand new pristine paddle steamer *Maid of the Loch* is at the main berth. (Douglas McGowan collection)

9 Still on Loch Lomond and this time, it's the majestic *Maid of the Loch* at Tarbet on 12 May 1972. The *Maid* was also a product of Inglis, built at their Pointhouse yard in 1953 and reassembled on the slipway at Balloch. Now owned by the Loch Lomond Steamship Company, their objective is to return her to service cruising on the Loch. (Lawrence Macduff).

10 A beautiful evocative view of Whiting Bay pier in 1961 with PS *Caledonia* alongside. Two red and cream coaches belonging to the local Whiting Bay bus company, A.C. Lennox, await their next turn of duty. Lennox's garage was just behind the photographer and was one of about 6 remaining independent companies on the island at that time. Quite remarkable for such a relatively small island. The pier closed at the end of the 1962 season. (Montague Smith)

11 MV *Maid of Argyll* on tendering duties to the Canadian Pacific liner *Empress of Britain* at the Tail of the Bank in the late 1950s. (Douglas McGowan collection)

12 Having crossed from Craigendoran and Gourock, PS *Jeanie Deans* arrives at Dunoon bound for Innellan, Rothesay and a cruise round Bute in July 1961. (Douglas McGowan collection)

13 The *Jeanie* makes a striking sight as she sweeps into Rothesay, August 1962. There is too much steam pressure in the boiler and the safety valves have lifted, causing the plume of white smoke to erupt from her forward funnel. (Richard Orr)

14 DEPV *Talisman* at Rothesay in September 1966. In only a few weeks, she would be withdrawn from service. (Douglas McGowan)

15 Winter hibernation at Queens Dock, Glasgow. Furthest from the camera are *Caledonia* and *Duchess of Hamilton* with *Waverley* and *Queen Mary II* nearest the camera. February 1968. (Douglas McGowan)

16 TS *King George V* completes the picture in Oban Bay at 8 a.m. on 6 July 1968. She has just left her overnight berth at the Railway Pier, swung around in the bay and is heading for the town's North Pier from which she will depart at 9.30 a.m. for her cruise to Iona. (Douglas McGowan)

17 A resplendent *King George V* arriving at Largs on a beautiful Spring morning, undertaking a special sailing for the Clyde River Steamer Club, 1 May 1971. (Douglas McGowan)

18 TS *King George V* passing Colintraive, on charter to the CSP Co and deputising for the *Queen Mary II* on 5 May 1971. (James Aikman Smith)

19 Passing the support piers for the new Erskine Bridge in the course of construction. *King George V* was sailing from Queens Dock, Glasgow, to Oban to start her 1969 season. The Erskine Ferry can just be seen on the left of the image taken May 1969. (Douglas McGowan)

20 Another view of *King George V* whilst under charter to the CSP Co. in May 1971. She is berthed unusually at Gourock with PS *Waverley* in the distance. (Douglas McGowan)

21 The *King George V* off Craigmore, Isle of Bute, on charter to the Clyde River Steamer Club, May 1974. (Lawrence Macduff)

22 *Right:* In a beautifully atmospheric scene, the Caledonian Steam Packet Company's paddle steamer *Mercury* berths at Rothesay pier on 24 July 1939. Only seventeen months later, she was damaged by a mine and consequently sank whilst under tow from Milford Haven to the Irish coast. (Clyde River Steamer Club).

23 *Below:* TS *Duchess of Hamilton*, with monastral blue hull and chocolate boot-topping, canting at Glasgow Bridge Wharf. It was unusual for the turbine steamers to turn at the King George V Bridge: usually they turned at Princes Dock and came upriver astern using the bow rudder. 15 September 1968. (Douglas McGowan)

24 Yet another fine day on the Clyde draws to a close as the evening sunshine falls on *Duchess of Hamilton* as she leaves Dunoon bound for Gourock on 8 June 1965. (Douglas McGowan)

25 The *Hamilton* at Inveraray on one of her Tuesday long-distance excursions in June 1969. (Douglas McGowan)

26 *Duchess of Hamilton* makes an attractive sight as she sweeps away from Rothesay, dressed overall for a charter sailing in the late 1950s. (Douglas McGowan collection)

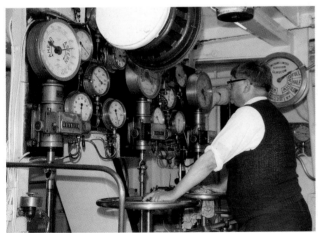

27 *Right:* Ned Higgins, Chief Engineer of *Duchess of Hamilton*. Although the turbine steamers did not have the spectacular engines of the paddlers to entertain the passengers, nevertheless, it was still interesting to watch the Engineer skillfully wrestle with the manoeuvring valves as the steamer came alongside a pier in August 1970. (Douglas McGowan)

28 *Above:* The engine-room of TS *Queen Mary II* in August 1970. (Douglas McGowan)

29 TS *Queen Mary II* departing from Largs in July 1970. Her masts have been shortened to allow her to pass under the Kingston Bridge which rather spoiled her appearance. (Douglas McGowan collection)

30 A view taken from MV *Maid of Ashton* showing *Queen Mary II* at Dunoon pier undertaking a special charter sailing in August 1970. (Douglas McGowan collection)

31 PS *Caledonia* approaching Gourock from Craigendoran in her final few weeks of service in August 1969. (Douglas McGowan)

32 It is a beautiful summer's day on Arran as *Caledonia* comes alongside Brodick, returning from her Monday cruise to Pladda in August 1965. (Douglas McGowan)

33 A Sunday morning at 9 a.m. in July 1976 at Glasgow's Anderston Quay, *Waverley's* 'home' berth. During the 1976 season, *Queen Mary II* (nearest the camera) sailed at 11 a.m. in direct competition to *Waverley* on Sundays. Although *Waverley* (seen here canting in the river) was forced to sail at the ludicrously early time of 9.30 a.m., she succeeded in attracting by far the lion's share of traffic. (Douglas McGowan)

34 PS *Waverley* sails majestically into Dunoon in July 1977. Tragically, a few days later, she was stranded on the Gantock rocks just a few hundred yards from where this photograph was taken. Fortunately, she was refloated later in the day and returned to service six weeks later after extensive repairs. (Douglas McGowan)

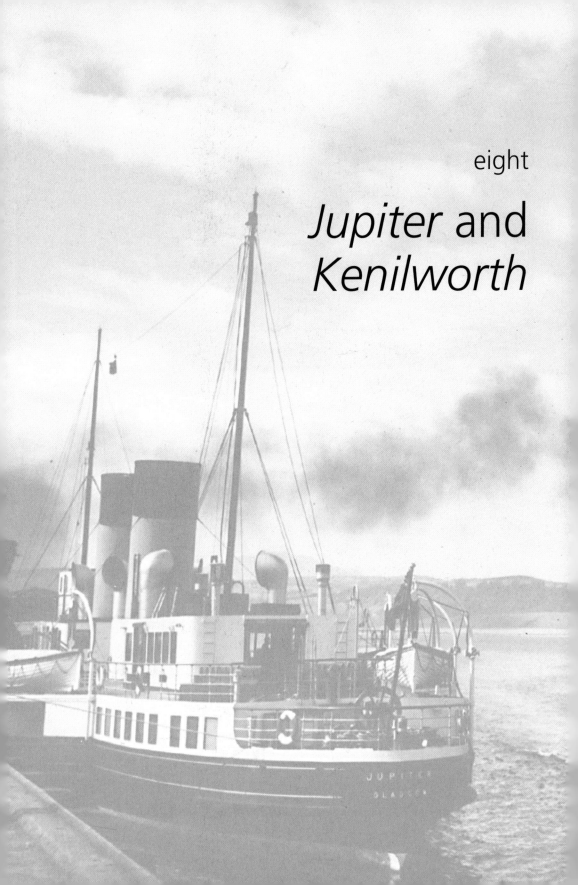

eight

Jupiter and *Kenilworth*

PS *Jupiter*, seen here leaving Rothesay in her first few weeks of service, was built by Fairfield's of Govan in 1937 for the Caledonian Steam Packet Co. She was a useful steamer during her relatively short career, with a large passenger capacity of 1,509 and stowage space for six cars. (Alexander Gray collection)

Jupiter in Rothesay Bay, September 1938. After only three seasons, she was requisitioned by the Admiralty at Milford Haven, then Dover, being renamed HMS *Scawfell*. She also made several trips to Holland and operated for a spell on the east coast between the Tyne and the Humber. She had distinguished war service and took part in the Normandy landings. (Alexander Gray collection)

PS *Jupiter* arriving back at her Gourock base in July 1938. Following the Second World War, she was refitted and returned to the Gourock–Wemyss Bay–Rothesay ferry routes. (Alexander Gray collection)

With the Gantock light on the left, *Jupiter* makes a stirring arrival at Dunoon in September 1938. (Alexander Gray collection)

Jupiter departing from Kirn on a July 1937 afternoon. A difficult ship to handle, she was slow to answer the helm and sometimes did the opposite of what was intended! (Alexander Gray collection)

Jupiter alongside Gourock with *Duchess of Fife* approaching in 1938. (Alexander Gray collection)

Jupiter approaches Dunoon in around 1939 with one of the LNER paddlers having just left, bound for Craigendoran. (Douglas Brown collection)

Jupiter berths at Rothesay in July 1948, the year of nationalization and also the year when much of the colour vanished from the Clyde: the 'standard' buff funnels with black tops of the CSP Co. would now reign supreme! MacBrayne's steamers' distinctive red and black funnels would however still add a little contrast to the scene. In this view, *Jupiter*'s anchor has been used to hold the bow steady and prevent her being blown against the pier during the berthing operation. Also, note the enclosed bridge, new for the 1948 season, with canvas dodgers. (Douglas McGowan collection)

Leaving Gourock on ferry duty to Dunoon, June 1956. For the 1956 season, she was converted to burn oil at a cost of £30,000, which was a not insignificant sum in the 1950s. (Douglas McGowan collection)

Jupiter leaving Innellan, *c*.1950. Although capable of 17 knots when built, by the 1950s she struggled to achieve 13 knots and she suffered from boiler and tube problems latterly. (Graham Langmuir collection)

For the 1957 season (which proved to be her last), she was employed on the Glasgow–Lochgoilhead Sunday cruise with various railway connection rosters on weekdays. She is seen here arriving at Lochgoilhead on a Sunday in August 1957. (Campbell Kerr collection)

On the same day in August 1957, *Jupiter* departs from Lochgoilhead astern, bound for Glasgow. Surprisingly, she was laid up just a few weeks later, after only twenty years service and having been in service for only twenty weeks following her expensive conversion to oil-burning the previous year. After languishing in the Albert Harbour, Greenock, for almost four years, she eventually left for Dublin under tow in 1961 for scrapping. The last steamer call at Lochgoilhead was made in July 1965 by MV *Maid of Skelmorlie*. (Campbell Kerr)

Sister-ship of *Talisman*, PS *Kenilworth* (above) was built in 1898 for the North British Railway Co. and was used mainly on the fast services to Rothesay from Craigendoran. Internally, she was luxuriously fitted out with a solid mahogany saloon and an aft saloon of oak, upholstered with sumptuous gold velvet. She is photographed here in July 1936. (Douglas McGowan collection)

During the First World War, *Kenilworth* was used as a minesweeper along with *Talisman* based at Troon harbour and latterly at Portsmouth. She was broken up in 1938. She is seen here in her final year of service. (Alexander Gray collection)

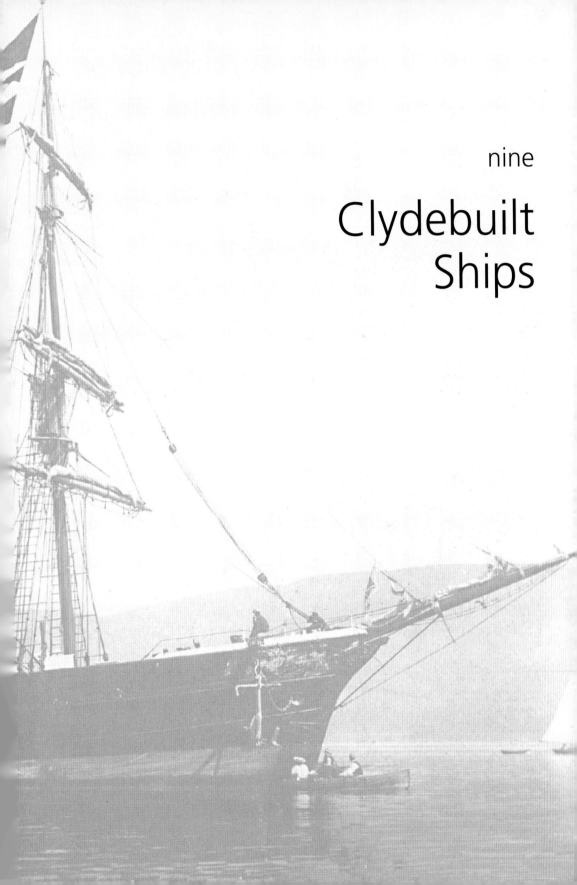

nine

Clydebuilt Ships

Cunard's magnificent *Lusitania*, on trials on the Clyde, June 1907. Built by John Brown's Clydebank yard, she was fitted with four Parsons steam turbines which were revolutionary at the time. She was 761 feet in length and weighed 31,000 gross tons and, along with *Mauretania*, was the first ship capable of crossing the Atlantic in under five days. She was torpedoed by a German submarine on 7 May 1915 as she was approaching the southern Irish coast. She sank in eighteen minutes and a total of 1,198 lives were lost. Along with the *Titanic* disaster, the sinking of the *Lusitania* is surrounded by more controversy than any other ship before or since. (Douglas McGowan collection)

SS *Lady Louth* (1,870 gross tons) was delivered by the Ardrossan Dockyard Co. in 1923 and she took up the nightly service between Dublin and Liverpool. In addition to cargo, she had accommodation for eighty first-class and ninety steerage passengers. (Douglas McGowan collection)

The Cunarder *Queen Mary* fitting out at Clydebank, 29 June 1935. A substantial amount of work remained to be done in the following ten months before she would be ready for her maiden voyage. The rusting hulk of 'number 534' had remained untouched for two years on the stocks at Clydebank, a victim of the worldwide recession of the early 1930s. (Douglas McGowan collection)

Some eight months later, the *Queen Mary* is seen here near completion. All three funnels have been fitted, the lifeboats and davits are all in position and the final coat of paint is being applied around the ship's stern. Very soon, she would leave the yard of her birth and complete her trials on the measured mile off the Island of Arran. (Douglas McGowan)

An interesting assortment of shipping at the 'Tail of the Bank', off Gourock. From left to right, SS *Davaar* is on a sightseeing cruise and is listing heavily to port; DEPV *Talisman* is similarly employed and is dressed with flags for the special occasion as she lists heavily to starboard; the centerpiece is of course the newly completed giant Cunarder *Queen Mary*, at anchor having come downriver from Clydebank prior to starting trials; the tug *Romsey* and finally, steaming off into the distance is the TS *Atalanta*. 26 March, 1936. (Douglas McGowan collection)

SS *Princess Victoria* was built in 1912 by Denny of Dumbarton for Portpatrick & Wigtownshire Railways for their Stranraer-Larne ferry service. During the First World War, she was used as a troopship, being finally withdrawn and sold to breakers in Norway in 1934. (Douglas McGowan collection)

SS *Viper* leaving Ardrossan, *c*.1912. Built by Fairfield's, she entered service in 1906 for Burns & Laird. On trials, she achieved 22 knots. She was sold to the Isle of Man Steam Packet Co in 1920. (Campbell McCutcheon collection)

When built in 1913, TS *Paris* was said to be the fastest ship of her type in the world. Used as a cross-Channel ferry, she was converted to a hospital ship during the Second World War, and took part in the Dunkirk evacuation. (Douglas McGowan collection)

Perhaps not the most attractive of Clydebuilt vessels, but interesting nevertheless, the twin-funnelled paddle vessel *Viena* of 1906 was built by A. & J. Inglis of Pointhouse for the Argentine Navigation Co. for service on the River Plate to Montevideo and the Parana up to Paraguay. Withdrawn in 1960, she was not finally scrapped until 1981. (Douglas McGowan collection)

Not actually 'Clydebuilt' but Auxiliary Steamer *Scotia* was formerly a Norwegian whaler refitted on the Clyde by the Scottish explorer William S. Bruce. Photographed off Gourock following the major Antarctic expedition of 1903. (Douglas McGowan collection)

SS *Windsor Castle*, 18,900 gross tons, was built in 1922 by John Brown & Co., Clydebank. She was sunk whilst in a convoy in March 1943 by a German torpedo 100 miles north-west of Algiers. (Douglas McGowan collection)

SS *Transylvania* was a product of the Fairfield yard at Govan and, with her three imposing funnels, made an attractive vessel. She entered service in 1925 for the Anchor Line and was used mainly on the transatlantic service to New York. She was torpedoed and sunk in 1940 by enemy action. (Douglas McGowan collection)

SS *Lhasa* was built in 1904 by Denny's for the British India Steam Navigation Co. for their UK–India service. She is seen here on trials off Arran in February 1905. (Douglas McGowan collection)

SS *Calgarian*, another product of the Fairfield yard, was a handsome, well-proportioned ship. She entered service on the Liverpool-Quebec service in 1914 but, attacked by a torpedo four years later, she sunk off Rathlin Island. (Douglas McGowan collection)

Another 'three funneller', TS *Queen of Bermuda* is seen here on trials on the Clyde on 14 February 1933. The third funnel was removed in 1940 to enable guns to be fitted. She carried many thousands of troops during the Second World War.

TS *Lama* (sister ship to *Lhasa*) was built in 1905 by Denny of Dumbarton for British India's Bombay-Karachi route. A triple screw steamer, she could carry thirty-nine first-class, twenty-two second-class and 1,164 deck passengers. She was an attractive ship with a tier of deckhouses amidships and aft, two well-raked masts and funnels and a pair of cowled Samson posts at the after end of the centre-castle. (Douglas McGowan collection)

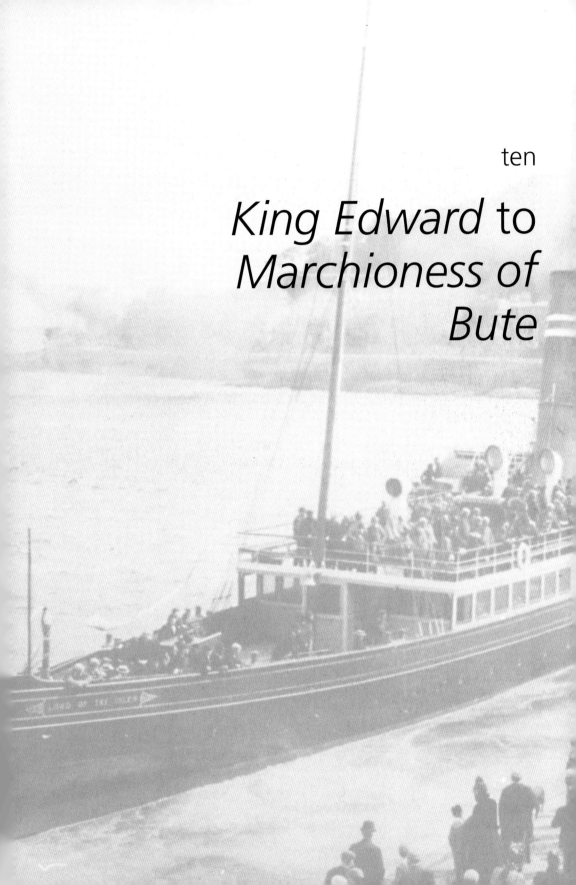

ten

King Edward to Marchioness of Bute

Owned originally by the Turbine Steamers syndicate, *King Edward* created history in 1901 as the world's first turbine passenger steamer. On trials, she achieved 20.45 knots and although she perhaps did not have the grace of the paddlers, she was nevertheless an attractive ship. *King Edward* was noticeably free of the rhythmic surging motion and vibration which was present in even the best of the paddle steamers of the era, a feature which no doubt contributed to her popularity with the travelling public. This view shows her arriving at Dunoon, June 1937. (Alexander Gray collection)

With not an inch of deck space to spare, *King Edward* in Rothesay Bay, July 1938. Her maximum capacity was 1,966 passengers. (Alexander Gray collection)

At first *King Edward* was placed on the Greenock Princes Pier-Dunoon-Rothesay-Fairlie-Lochranza-Campbeltown service and then on the Inveraray run. In 1915, she was requisitioned and served as a troopship in the Channel Islands and various Channel ports. After the war, she returned to her familiar haunts on the Clyde. (Alexander Gray collection)

In 1927, she passed to Williamson-Buchanan ownership and operated Glasgow-Rothesay-Arran excursions. She completed her career as a CSP Co. vessel and she is seen here at the Broomielaw, Glasgow in 1951 preparing for her 10 a.m. sailing 'doon the watter' on what was probably her last ever sailing. The bow of *Queen Mary II* is on the left. (Douglas McGowan collection)

A superb view of TS *King George V* at speed off Gourock in the early 1930s. This fine steamer also had her place in history as the first passenger steamer to be fitted with high pressure steam turbines. Like *King Edward*, the *George* was built by Denny of Dumbarton, joining the Turbine Steamers fleet late in 1926. She incorporated a number of improvements on her predecessor by being the first Clyde steamer to have part of her promenade deck enclosed and her dining saloon situated on the main deck aft. She was usually to be seen on the Campbeltown and Inveraray rosters. (Douglas McGowan collection)

Reboilered for the second time in 1935, she was fitted with new, larger funnels and at the same time passed into the ownership of David MacBrayne Ltd. For the rest of her career, she was to be mainly associated with the Staffa and Iona cruise from Oban. She is seen here with her new funnels, but still with 'open' bridge off Gourock in around 1936. (Douglas McGowan collection)

King George V makes a very rare appearance at Glasgow Bridge Wharf as she berths, flags flying, ready to take a special party downriver on 2 June 1956. (Douglas McGowan collection)

A classic view of *King George V* in Oban Bay bound for Tobermory, Staffa and Iona, July 1962. Cruises to Staffa were discontinued after the 1968 season following an alleged rockfall. Interestingly, she was chartered by the CSP Co. in 1971 to deputise for *Queen Mary II* whilst the latter was having a major facelift at Barclay, Curle's yard. The veteran MacBrayne turbine flew the Caley pennant during this period but her funnels steadfastly remained MacBrayne red! She was withdrawn after the 1974 season, eventually being towed to Cardiff where work commenced to convert her to a floating restaurant, but she met the same fate as her former Clyde consort *Caledonia* and was destroyed by fire. (Campbell Kerr)

SS *Kinloch* was built in 1878 by A. & J. Inglis Ltd for the Clyde & Campbeltown Shipping Company. She was the first (and presumably the last) Clyde steamer to have a separate wheelhouse, situated under the navigating bridge. However, this was removed shortly after entering service on safety grounds. This view shows her at Carradale, in the Kilbrannan Sound. The pier was opened in 1870 and closed to steamer traffic in 1940. (A Fraser)

Although this paddler was launched in 1897 as *Kylemore* for Captain Williamson, she was actually purchased prior to completion by the Hastings, St Leonards-on-Sea and Eastbourne Steamboat Co. who renamed her *Britannia*. In 1904, she returned to Williamson but almost immediately was renamed *Vulcan* and transferred to the Glasgow & South Western fleet. (Alexander Gray collection)

Seen here near Dunoon *c.*1936. Yet another change in ownership occurred in April 1908 when she returned to Captain Williamson, and her original name, *Kylemore*, was restored, plying on the Glasgow-Rothesay route. (Alexander Gray collection)

Kylemore setting off downriver from Glasgow on one of her regular sailings to Rothesay, summer 1937. During the First World War, she was on minesweeping duties at Dunkirk and then Harwich. (Alexander Gray collection)

Along with the other Williamson Buchanan steamers, *Kylemore* passed to her final owners, the Caledonian Steam Packet Co. in 1935. In her second period of war service, she was sunk by enemy action off Harwich in 1940. (Alexander Gray collection)

Entering service in 1891, this little North British paddler, *Lady Clare*, was principally employed on the Gareloch and Greenock-Craigendoran commuter and ferry services. Sold off the Clyde in 1906, she was based at Belfast during the First World War, and was scrapped at Dumbarton in 1928. (Douglas McGowan collection)

Two small motor vessels, the *Ashton* and *Leven* (the latter seen here in 1938), were launched by Denny of Dumbarton in 1938, with the objective of carrying passengers from Glasgow to view the shipyards during the Empire Exhibition which was staged in the city. *Leven* spent her final Clyde years mainly on the Largs-Millport and other short ferry routes. (Douglas McGowan collection)

Built in 1931, *Lochfyne* was unique; she was the first British passenger vessel to have her propellers driven by direct-coupled electric motors receiving their power from diesel engines. Post-war, she spent most of her summers based at Oban, assisting *King George V* on day excursions. Between 1959 and 1969, she was based on the Clyde on the Tarbert and Ardrishaig service. Excessive noise and vibration could be experienced throughout the ship. She is seen here arriving at Tarbert at 12.30 p.m. on a beautiful Autumn day, 25 September 1937. (Alexander Gray collection)

PS *Lord of the Isles* (*I*) was built in 1877 by D. & W. Henderson of Meadowside for the Glasgow & Inveraray Steamboat Co.'s Inveraray service. Look at the crowds lining Rothesay pier in addition to those already on board *Lord of the Isles*! Captured by the camera *c*. 1896. (Campbell McCutcheon collection)

PS *Lord of the Isles* (*II*) in Rothesay Bay in the early 1900s. She was owned by the Glasgow & Inveraray Steamboat Co., and in 1891, she introduced a new standard of luxury, not previously seen to the Clyde fleet. (Douglas McGowan collection)

Above: PS *Lord of the Isles* (*II*) was placed on the prestigious 180-mile daily return sailing from Glasgow to Inveraray. Her internal furnishings were of a very high standard, as were her catering facilities. She was eventually acquired by Turbine Steamers Ltd and transferred to the Glasgow-Round Bute excursion. By 1928, she had become too expensive to operate and at the end of that season was broken up by Smith & Houston, Port Glasgow. She is seen here in around 1905 sailing majestically into Rothesay bay. (Douglas McGowan collection)

Below: PS *Lucy Ashton* was built by the yard of Tommy Seath at Rutherglen in 1888 and she was to become one of the best-loved and famous Clyde steamers of all time. She was owned by the North British Steam Packet Co. and operated the Holy Loch service but later transferred to the Gareloch route based at Craigendoran. This view shows her steaming into Rothesay in 1937. (Alexander Gray collection)

PS *Lucy Ashton* was one of the few Clyde paddlers not 'called up' in 1939 and gave sterling service for over six years. However, ironically when this photograph was taken at Craigendoran, she was out of service for repairs. Meanwhile, PS *Fair Maid* (ex *Isle of Skye*, ex *Madge Wildfire*) has taken up *Lucy*'s roster and is seen leaving the pier, bound for Dunoon, in Spring 1944. (Douglas McGowan collection)

PS *Lucy Ashton* laid up at Bowling Harbour 1949, the year she was withdrawn from service and broken up at Faslane, after distinguished service of over sixty years. Her long career was not quite over: her hull was used by the British Shipbuilding and Research Association for resistance tests and she was fitted with jet propulsion engines. The hull was finally disposed of in 1951. (Douglas McGowan collection)

MV *Maid of Cumbrae* was one of four small motor vessels built in 1953, (*Maid of Skelmorlie, Ashton, Argyll* and *Cumbrae*), all of which were virtually identical. They were introduced to replace some of the older, more expensive paddlers and were used for short cruises and ferry work. Although undoubtedly very useful vessels in the fleet, with a passenger capacity of only 625, they were unable to move the large volumes of passengers which their steam counterparts had previously done with ease. She is photographed here leaving Rothesay with PS Waverley on charter to the Paddle Steamer Preservation Society, already under way, September 1971. (Douglas McGowan)

PS *Marchioness of Breadalbane* departs from Rothesay in the late 1920s. She was launched from the yard of John Reid & Co. of Paisley in 1890 for the CSP Co. and was based at Wemyss Bay operating various ferry services. During the First World War, she was on minesweeping duties in the English Channel. (Clyde River Steamer Club)

PS *Marchioness of Bute* at Gourock pier, 1907. She was a sister-ship of the *Marchioness of Breadalbane* and was similarly based at Wemyss Bay. A year after this photograph was taken, she was sold for excursion work on the Firth of Tay. (Douglas McGowan collection)

PS *Marchioness of Bute* leaving Newburgh on the River Tay, *c*.1909. Built by John Reid & Co. in 1890, she operated mainly out of Wemyss Bay. In 1908, she was sold for excursions on the River Tay, being finally laid up at Inverkeithing and broken up in 1923. (Douglas McGowan collection)

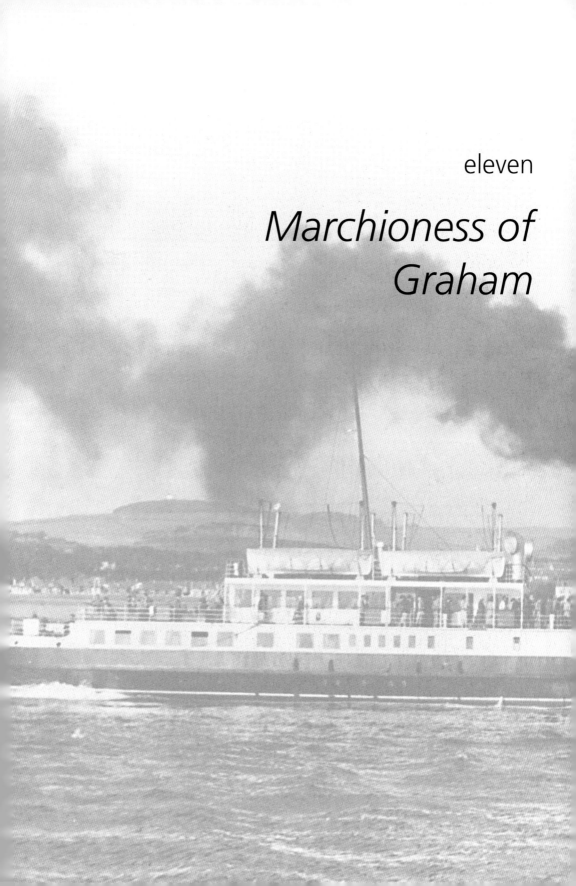

eleven

Marchioness of Graham

TS *Marchioness of Graham* replaced the first generation turbine steamer *Atalanta* on the Ardrossan–Arran run in 1936. Built by Fairfield's of Govan for the Caledonian Steam Packet Co., she was fitted with four turbines driving twin screws through single reduction gearing. She is seen here alongside Lochgoilhead pier in July 1950. (Douglas McGowan collection)

By the end of the 1957 season, the *Marchioness* was the only vessel in the CSP Co. fleet to be coal-fired, obvious in this view of her arriving at Ardrossan from Whiting Bay, July 1957! She had a passenger capacity of 1,300 and space for up to ten cars. (Campbell Kerr)

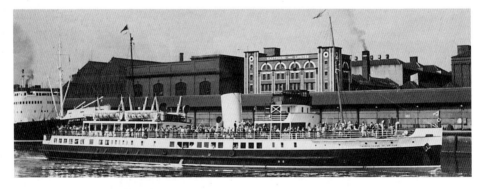

On a 1957 up-river August excursion to Glasgow, she passes the Kingston Dock. During the Second World War, she worked on passenger services on the Clyde. From 1947, Ayr became her base, although she returned to the Ardrossan–Arran haunts of her youth at peak periods. During her final five years of service, she was used almost exclusively on the Arran ferry services, replacing the turbine *Glen Sannox*. In 1958, she was withdrawn from service and sold for further service in Greece where a very substantial refit made her unrecognisable. (Campbell Kerr)

twelve

Marchioness of Lorne to *Queen-Empress*

With flags proudly flying, PS *Marchioness of Lorne* is launched by the Fairfield Shipbuilding & Engineering Co., Govan in 1935. Never the most glamorous or outstanding of the Clyde steamers with a rather squat funnel, the 'wee Lorne', as she was affectionately known by her regulars, was built for the Holy Loch run. (Campbell McCutcheon collection)

PS *Marchioness of Lorne* leaving Gourock, shortly after entering service in 1935. Note the open bridge, which continued until after the war. (Douglas McGowan collection)

A delightful view of *Marchioness of Lorne* off Gourock, 1951. Note the enclosed bridge but canvas dodgers still in position. Despite the impressive bow wave, she struggled to achieve 12 knots in service and consequently acquired a reputation for being the 'slow boat to China'. Despite this, during her short (twenty year) career, she proved to be a sturdy and reliable member of the fleet. (Douglas McGowan collection)

Marchioness of Lorne, flags flying, on a special sailing from Largs, June 1951. MV *Leven* is berthed at the side of the pier on Millport ferry duties. (Douglas McGowan collection)

PS *Marchioness of Lorne* off Gourock in 1953. She was withdrawn in 1955 and sold to the British Iron & Steel Corporation (Salvage) Ltd but broken up by Smith and Houston, Port Glasgow, on their behalf. (Alexander Gray collection)

PS *Marmion*, seen here in the evening sunshine in 1937, entered service for the North British Steam Packet Co. in 1906, built mainly for the Arrochar excursion trade from Craigendoran, replacing *Redgauntlet*. (Alexander Gray collection)

Marmion was designed for all-year round service. During the First World War, she was based at Dover, carrying out minesweeping duties in the English Channel, and returning to the Clyde in 1920. This view shows her arriving at Dunoon in August 1938. (Alexander Gray collection)

Leaving Dunoon, June 1939. In 1932, *Marmion* was reboiled and underwent an extensive refit. She was 'called up' for war service in September 1939 for her second spell of minesweeping, this time based at Harwich. She made three voyages to the beaches of Dunkirk but was sunk during an air attack in April 1941. (Douglas McGowan collection)

It's 4.50 p.m. on 3 September 1938 and *Marmion* makes a stirring sight as she approaches Kirn on her return leg to Craigendoran. (Alexander Gray collection)

PS *Mars* was yet another product of the famous John Brown yard in 1902 for the Glasgow & South Western Railway Co. Sadly, she was run down by a destroyer in 1918 whilst minesweeping off Harwich. (Douglas McGowan collection)

PS *Mercury* (*I*) was built in 1892, another G&SWR steamer, and was primarily employed on the Kyles of Bute service. She is pictured here arriving at Rothesay in the early 1900s. (Douglas McGowan collection)

PS *Mercury* had some spectacular exploits during the First World War: she had her stern blown off when she struck a mine off the east coast of England. Then, following repairs and after only one day back in service, she struck another mine and had her bow blown off! She was again repaired and gave sterling Clyde service until withdrawn in 1933. This view shows her leaving the Clyde for war service, repainted as number 578 in wartime grey, in around 1916. (Douglas McGowan collection)

An exciting early 1930s view of *Mercury* racing TS *Duchess of Montrose* off Craigmore, as they both make a bid to be first into Rothesay. (Douglas McGowan collection)

The paddle steamers *Caledonia* and *Mercury* (*II*) were both similar in appearance and entered service for the CSP Co. in 1934. *Mercury*, seen here, was built by Fairfield's. This view shows her sweeping into Largs, June 1937. (Alexander Gray collection)

PS *Mercury* leaving Dunoon, August 1938. Rather than the traditional style of paddlebox with vents, the sponsons were continuous and a white box platform above the deck was all that distinguished the *Caledonia* and *Mercury* from their turbine cousins. This gave passengers the impression of speed and modernity. (Douglas McGowan collection)

Mercury off Gourock, June 1939. Only a few months later she was requisitioned by the Admiralty for minesweeping duties and sank whilst under tow between Milford Haven and the Irish coast in December 1940. (Alexander Gray collection)

Clouds of black smoke as the Glasgow & South Western Railway's PS *Minerva* (1893) approaches Rothesay, returning from the Kyles of Bute in the early 1900s. (Douglas McGowan collection)

PS *Pioneer* was another A. & J. Inglis product, built in 1905 specifically for MacBrayne's Islay service from West Loch Tarbert. She was fully plated forward up to the promenade deck to withstand the rigours of winter crossings to Islay. This view shows her arriving at West Loch Tarbert from Port Ellen, September 1937. (Alexander Gray collection)

A pleasant perspective of *Pioneer* as she completes her cant at the West Loch. She has already swung round and is being hauled in by means of the cant rope which can be seen protruding from the bow. Very few passengers are in evidence on this day, 14 September 1937. (Alexander Gray collection)

Pioneer's paddle wheels were smaller than usual and her draught less than normal, the reason being the very shallow waters around West Loch Tarbert, particularly at spring tides. *Pioneer* proved to be a very reliable unit of the MacBrayne fleet during her long career. She is seen here canting at West Loch Tarbert, in around 1935. (Campbell Kerr)

The postmark on this card is 22 August 1933 but the photograph probably dates back to the late 1920s and shows TS *Queen Alexandra II* (later *Saint Columba*) slowing down at Pirnmill, Isle of Arran, en route to Campbeltown, and about to ferry passengers ashore. *Queen Alexandra* was a fine turbine steamer, used mainly on the Campbeltown service from 1912 by her owners, Turbine Steamers Ltd. (Douglas McGowan collection)

PS *Queen-Empress* was built in 1912 for John Williamson's fleet and was one of the few Clyde steamers built by the Port Glasgow yard of Messrs Murdoch and Murray. Following war service as a troop transport and then minesweeper based on the Tyne, she resumed Clyde services and by the early 1920s had become a permanent feature on the Glasgow-Rothesay and Lochgoilhead runs. (Alexander Gray collection)

A crowded *Queen-Empress* arriving at Rothesay on 10 August 1938. Two years earlier, she had been transferred to the Caledonian fleet and was used on railway connection services from the main terminals. On return from her second period of war service in 1946, it was not considered worthwhile refitting her and she was subsequently sold to Dutch breakers in August 1946. (Douglas McGowan collection)

thirteen

Queen Mary/ Queen Mary II

Launched as *Queen Mary* by Denny of Dumbarton in 1933 for Williamson-Buchanan, she was slightly shorter but broader than her Gourock-based *Duchess* counterparts and she had excellent passenger capacity of 2,086. She immediately took over from *King Edward* on the 10 a.m. run from Glasgow to the Clyde Coast. (Alexander Gray collection)

Queen Mary retained the two-class accommodation and her observation lounge on the forward promenade deck was beautifully fitted out, right up to the end of her sea-going career. Powered by a Scotch boiler and direct-acting turbines with three propellers, she achieved almost 20 knots on trials. Both views on this page show her leaving Glasgow in 1937 with two funnels and one mast, as built. (Alexander Gray collection)

Interestingly, she was renamed *Queen Mary II* in 1935 to allow her original name to be used for the new Cunarder which was then fitting out at Clydebank. She is seen here sweeping away from Dunoon on her way back upriver, August 1953. (Campbell Kerr)

The *Mary* passed into CSP Co. ownership in 1935, her white funnels becoming yellow with black tops. During the Second World War, she remained on the Clyde, her time spent almost entirely on the Gourock-Dunoon ferry service.. She was fitted with a mainmast in 1953, as seen above. (Alexander Gray collection)

TS *Queen Mary II* makes a fine sight as she arrives back at Rothesay in July 1955 from her daily cruise to Tighnabruaich. (Douglas McGowan collection)

TS *Queen Mary II* passing Govan Ferry, June 1954. The *Mary* endeared herself to Glaswegians over the years who adopted her as 'their' boat. (Campbell Kerr)

In the spring of 1957, *Queen Mary II* was reboilered and the opportunity was taken at the same time to replace her two funnels with one large elliptical funnel. She was still, nevertheless, a handsome vessel. She was the fleet's flagship during the 1950s. Seen here shortly after her refit and now sporting one funnel in June 1957, arriving back at Bridge Wharf, Glasgow. The King George V bridge is in the background, proclaiming advertisements for 'Capstan' and 'India Tyres'! (Campbell Kerr)

Latterly, *Queen Mary II* was based at Gourock following the withdrawal of regular sailings from Glasgow at the end of the 1969 season. She took over many of the former *Duchess of Hamilton*'s rosters including Inveraray and Campbeltown and even some additional Saturday afternoon cruises round Ailsa Craig. This view shows her arriving at Gourock from Glasgow in August 1967. PS *Caledonia* can be spotted on the left, making her way across from Craigendoran for her own afternoon cruise. (Douglas McGowan)

In 1975 and 1976, competition again returned to the Clyde as *Waverley* was returned to service by the Paddle Steamer Preservation Society operating as Waverley Steam Navigation Co. Ltd. *Queen Mary* (she had reverted to her original name in 1976) proved to be no match for the slick marketing campaign behind *Waverley*'s return to service. Despite Caledonian MacBrayne basing her at Glasgow at weekends in 1976 in face to face competition with the paddler, it became obvious that there was only sufficient traffic remaining for one vessel to survive. *Queen Mary* was therefore withdrawn from service at the end of the 1977 season. After a gap of some years when she languished in a London dock, she was eventually converted to a floating pub/restaurant in London in 1989, where today she happily survives, again sporting two funnels and the last representative of a Clyde turbine steamer. She is seen here leaving Inveraray on special charter, with *Duchess of Hamilton* alongside the pier in June 1968. (Douglas McGowan)

PS *Redgauntlet* entered service in 1895 for the North British Railway Co. This fine little paddler was mainly to be seen on the Craigendoran-Rothesay service, and later on various cruising duties. (Douglas McGowan collection)

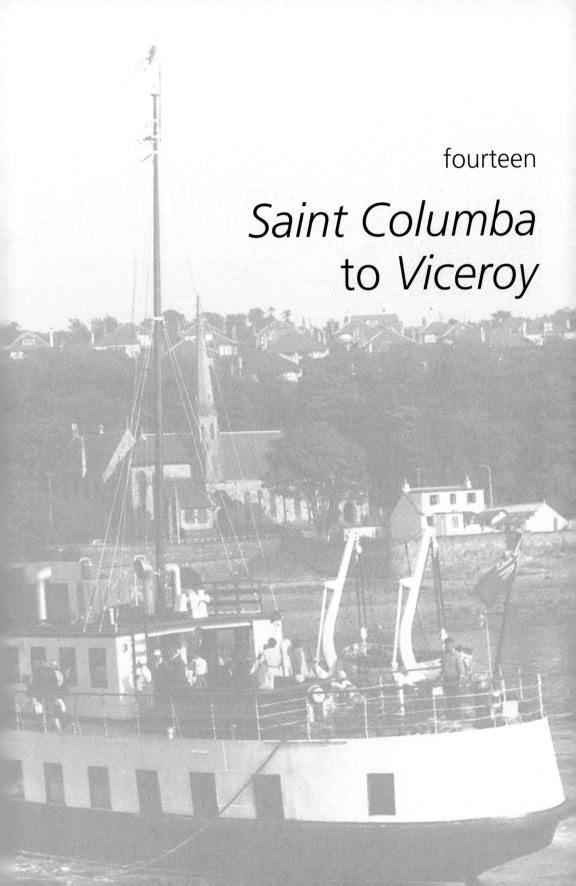

fourteen

Saint Columba to *Viceroy*

In 1935, the LMS Railway Co. (in association with David MacBrayne Ltd) acquired Williamson-Buchanan Steamers and Turbine Steamers Ltd. The 'assets' of Williamson-Buchanan included the fine turbine steamer *Queen Alexandra*, and her funnels were soon changed from white to red with black tops. However, when she re-entered service in 1936, she had a completely different profile. The promenade deck had been extended aft and a third funnel and mainmast added. The refurbished steamer was named *Saint Columba* and her new appearance was rather majestic and pleasing to the eye. Here, she is photographed going astern from Tarbert Loch Fyne, August 1938. (Alexander Gray collection)

TS *Saint Columba* was the only Clyde steamer to have three funnels and was regularly employed on the Glasgow-Ardrishaig route, departing at 7.11 a.m., like her illustrious predecessor, *Columba*. She was able to carry a maximum of 1,800 passengers. She is seen here approaching Dunoon, September 1938. (Alexander Gray collection)

Leaving Tarbert Loch Fyne, July 1937. During the First World War, *Saint Columba* was berthed in the East India harbour, Greenock and used as an accommodation ship for boom defence personnel. She went through a major refit in 1947, returning to her old Loch Fyne pre-war haunts during that summer. (Alexander Gray collection)

Having disembarked her passengers, *Saint Columba* leaves Gourock and heads upriver to her overnight berth at Greenock. One of the brand new Maid-class vessels can be seen on the left, crossing from Craigendoran in August 1953. (Douglas McGowan collection)

A packed *Saint Columba* draws into Dunoon, *c.*1955. Even in the twilight of her career, she was still able to approach her pre-war speed of 21 knots. Her sharp bow cut through the water with ease and if challenged by one of the *Duchesses*, she seldom lost the battle! (Douglas McGowan collection)

Saint Columba arriving at Innellan, 2 September 1953. Faced with the threat of closure in 1949 and 1952, the last official call at Innellan was by PS *Waverley* on 30 September 1972. However, between March and October 1974, it reopened briefly to convey workers to the Ardyne oil rig construction yard. (Douglas McGowan collection)

Saint Columba sailed until the end of the 1958 season, being sold and broken up by Smith & Houston of Port Glasgow the following year. This delightful view shows her passing another MacBrayne vessel, MV *Lochshiel* (built in 1929, sold in 1952) in the river off Greenock, June 1949. (Montague Smith)

PS *Scotia* and PS *Vivid* at Glasgow in the early 1880s. *Scotia* is the two-funnelled vessel nearest the camera and has departed downriver. A member of the Buchanan fleet and mainly used on the Ardrossan-Arran service, she became a G&SWR steamer in 1891. PS *Vivid* was built in 1864 for Captain Campbell's Kilmun service and was closely associated with the Rothesay route. She was the last operating Clyde steamer to have a steeple engine. (Campbell McCutcheon collection)

PS *Talisman* (*I*) in Rothesay Bay, 23 July 1929. Ordered by the North British Steam Packet Co. and launched in March 1896, *Talisman* achieved 18.7 knots on trials and gave sterling service over thirty-nine years, mainly on the Rothesay and Kyles roster. (Leo Vogt)

With the introduction of DEPV *Talisman* (*II*) to the LNER fleet in 1935, came a unique mode of propulsion for she was the first direct-acting diesel electric paddle vessel in the world. But she had a chequered career. She was caught by the camera off Kirn in July 1937. (Alexander Gray collection)

DEPV *Talisman* awaiting her next lot of passengers at Craigendoran, 1938. About a year after this photograph was taken, she was requisitioned by the Admiralty for war service, refitted as a gunship in 1940 and renamed HMS *Aristocrat*. She acquitted herself well as an anti-aircraft ship on the Thames, returning to the Clyde in 1946. (Douglas McGowan collection)

Although she was refurbished by A. & J. Inglis after the war, she was taken out of service and laid up after only seven years, as her diesel engines were in poor condition. However, she gained a late reprieve and was re-engined with British Polar Diesels, reappearing in June 1954. Although difficult to handle, probably due to her small rudder, and suffering from noise and vibration, she was economical and could be quickly rushed into service, without the need to raise steam over twenty-four hours. This view shows her leaving Dunoon for Wemyss Bay, June 1952. (Campbell Kerr)

Her second 'incarnation' saw her on the Wemyss Bay-Millport ferry service although she occasionally returned to her former base at Craigendoran for various excursions. In this interesting 1955 view of *Talisman*, she is tendering from Greenock Princes Pier to one of the Cunarders, possibly *Ivernia* or *Saxonia*, seen on the left at anchor at the tail of the bank on the voyage from Liverpool to Canada. On the right is one of the Canadian Pacific liners, either *Empress of Canada* or *Empress of Britain*. One of the other CSP Co. paddlers, possibly *Jupiter* or *Waverley*, would be on tendering duties to the *Empress*. The *Talisman*'s passenger capacity of 1,252 would come in handy on such rosters. This was a busy day at Princes Pier! (Campbell McCutcheon collection)

DEPV *Talisman* berthing at Wemyss Bay, August 1962. Her final season, 1966, was a painful one; due to lack of availability of spare parts, she ran for much of the season on only three out of four engines, sometimes at less than 10 knots with a knock-on effect on her timekeeping. She was withdrawn at the end of October and sold to W.H. Arnott Young & Co. for breaking up in the following year. (Douglas McGowan collection)

This evocative view shows PS *Viceroy* (nearest the camera) and owned by Captain Williamson (Snr) and PS *Victoria* of the Wemyss Bay Steamboat Co. racing off the Cowal shore, in about 1889. (Douglas McGowan collection)

fifteen

Waverley

PS *Waverley (III)*, when constructed in 1899, was the largest of her North British companions and unlike the rest was fitted with compound diagonal machinery. With her (almost) 20 knots, she was a real flier and often raced competitors *Jupiter* and *Duchess of Rothesay*. She seldom lost! *Waverley* is nearest the camera with PS *Iona* berthed alongside at Arrochar in the 1920s. (Douglas McGowan collection)

Above: Arriving back at Dunoon in 1937, with hardly a passenger in sight! Following the First World War, she was placed on the Loch Long and Arrochar roster as well as the Craigendoran-Rothesay commuter runs. (Alexander Gray collection)

Right: One of the relatively few Clyde steamers to see Admiralty service in both World Wars, in 1939, she became HMS *Waverley* and was converted for minesweeping duties again, this time based at Harwich. She is seen here again at Dunoon in the late 1930s. (Alexander Gray collection)

Leaving Lochgoilhead, 1920s. *Waverley* was involved in the evacuation of Dunkirk in May 1940, and in spite of heavy enemy gunfire, rescued several hundred troops from the beaches. Sadly, the gallant little paddler was badly damaged by a bomb and her steering gear put out of action. Shortly afterwards, she was struck amidships by yet another bomb and quickly sank. (Douglas McGowan collection)

In this photograph, which was taken around 1938, the *Waverley* is leaving a nice trail of black smoke as she sets off down Loch Long. (Alexander Gray collection)

One of the many rescued when *Waverley* went down at Dunkirk was her Captain, John Cameron, who became Master of the new *Waverley* in 1947. Long after his retirement, John followed the paddler's fortunes with great enthusiasm in her early years of preservation. Her predecessor is seen here in the 1920s. (Douglas McGowan collection)

Built to replace her illustrious predecessor, the new *Waverley* was built in 1947 by A. & J. Inglis for the LNER. Although it was probably anticipated at the time that *Waverley* would be the last paddle steamer built for Clyde service, no-one could ever have anticipated the remarkable career which would follow some thirty years later. Here she is seen approaching Largs on charter to the Paddle Steamer Preservation Society in May 1972. (John Goss)

In the winter of 1954-55, *Waverley* was converted from coal to oil burning and three years later, fitted with radar. By the early 1970s, she had become the last sea-going paddle steamer in the world and as such, a major focus of members of the PSPS. She is seen here sporting red and black funnels in 1973 which was to be her final year of operation for Caledonian MacBrayne Ltd. (John Goss)

After *Waverley*'s withdrawal in 1973, she was offered to the PSPS for the nominal sum of £1, the formal change of ownership to Waverley Steam Navigation Co. Ltd taking place in 1974. A public appeal arousing considerable public and media interest in the west of Scotland followed. As a result, the steamer was dry-docked, overhauled and returned to service in May 1975. She is seen here in her first days of preservation alongside Millport pier with *Keppel* arriving from Largs, 26 May 1975. (John Goss)

Although her home will always be the Clyde, *Waverley* has also been regularly visiting the Thames, Solent and Bristol Channel areas for some twenty-five years. Having benefitted from a £7 million extensive rebuild during the winters of 1999/2000 and 2002/2003, *Waverley* is set fair to give pleasure to thousands for many years to come. Without doubt, as the very last of the line, she is the most famous Clydebuilt steamer of all time, a household name not only in her home waters of the Firth of Clyde but also in all the other areas of the UK in which she operates. It is surely fitting that she is the last Clyde steamer to feature in this photographic collection – for it is *Waverley* alone which continues the link with the glorious traditions of the past for future generations to enjoy and appreciate.

Other local titles published by Tempus

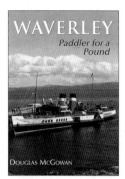

Waverley Paddler for a Pound

DOUGLAS McGOWAN

Waverley, the world's last sea-going paddle steamer, was destined for the scrap yard in 1974 when Douglas McGowan and the Paddle Steamer Preservation Society purchased her for the princely sum of £1 and the rest is, as they say, history. Fresh from a £7 million refit in Great Yarmouth, *Waverley* is resplendent in her black, red and white livery and can be seen sailing the coast of Britain again.

0 7524 2877 2

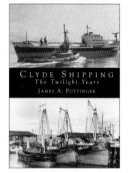

Clyde Shipping The Twilight Years

JAMES POTTINGER

Clyde Shipping – The Twilight Years is a trip down memory lane for those who remember when the Clyde was the third most important river in Britain and its ports some of the busiest. That heyday has gone and all that we have to remind us of the greatness of the Clyde are images such as the ones contained within this book.

0 7524 2138 7

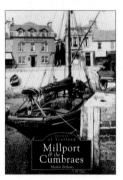

Millport & the Cumbraes

MARTIN BELLAMY

The history of Millport and the Cumbraes is rich and varied. For many people the mention of Millport conjures up images of the heady days of the Clyde as a holiday paradise with its pleasant climate, friendly atmosphere and wide range of attractions. Today it remains one of the best preserved Victorian towns in Scotland and Millport & the Cumbraes is a unique testament to the history of the town and the Cumbrae islands.

0 7524 2790 3

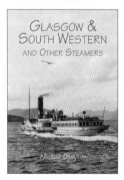

Glasgow & South Western and Other Steamers

ALISTAIR DEAYTON

Within the pages of Glasgow & South Western Railway Steamers are over 200 images of the fleet in its heyday, along with views of the ships of the Campbeltown & Glasgow Steam Packet Joint Stock Co. and Clyde Cargo Steamers Ltd and a handful of other operators who have played a small but important part in the history of shipping on the Clyde.

0 7524 2773 3

If you are interested in purchasing other books published by Tempus, or in case you have difficulty finding any Tempus books in your local bookshop, you can also place orders directly through our website

www.tempus-publishing.com

or from   **BOOKPOST**, Freepost, PO Box 29, Douglas, Isle of Man, IM99 1BQ
tel 01624 836000   email bookshop@enterprise.net